WORLD HISTORY Need to Know

The Cold War

by Daniel R. Faust

Consultant: Caitlin Krieck, Social Studies Teacher and Instructional Coach, The Lab School of Washington

Minneapolis, Minnesota

Credits

Cover and title page, © HUNG CHIN LIU/iStock; 5, © Vincent Grebenicek/Shutterstock; 7, © Keystone/ Getty Images; 9, © Print Collector/Getty Images; 11T, © Mariia Boiko/Shutterstock; 11B, © FotograFFF/ Shutterstock; 13, © Retro AdArchives/Alamy; 15, © David Turnley/Getty Images; 17, © Leif Skoogfors/ Getty Images; 19, © Keystone, MPI/Getty Images; 21, © Gwengoat/iStock; 23, © MPI/Getty Images; 25, © - / Contributor/Getty Images; 27, © Tom Stoddart Archive/Getty Images.

Bearport Publishing Company Product Development Team

President: Jen Jenson; Director of Product Development: Spencer Brinker; Managing Editor: Allison Juda; Associate Editor: Naomi Reich; Associate Editor: Tiana Tran; Senior Designer: Colin O'Dea; Designer: Elena Klinkner; Designer: Kayla Eggert; Product Development Assistant: Owen Hamlin

A NOTE FROM THE PUBLISHER: Some of the historic photos in this book have been colorized to help readers have a more meaningful and rich experience. The color results are not intended to depict actual historical detail.

STATEMENT ON USAGE OF GENERATIVE ARTIFICIAL INTELLIGENCE
Bearport Publishing remains committed to publishing high-quality nonfiction books. Therefore, we restrict the use of generative AI to ensure accuracy of all text and visual components pertaining to a book's subject. See BearportPublishing.com for details.

Library of Congress Cataloging-in-Publication Data

Names: Faust, Daniel R., author.
Title: The Cold War / Daniel R. Faust.
Description: Minneapolis, Minnesota : Bearport Publishing Company, [2024] |
    Series: World history : need to know | Includes bibliographical
    references and index.
Identifiers: LCCN 2023031023 (print) | LCCN 2023031024 (ebook) | ISBN
    9798889165514 (library binding) | ISBN 9798889165583 (paperback) | ISBN
    9798889165644 (ebook)
Subjects: LCSH: Cold War–Juvenile literature. | World
    politics–1945–1989–Juvenile literature. | United States–Foreign
    relations–1945–1989–Juvenile literature. | Soviet Union–Foreign
    relations–1945–1991–Juvenile literature.
Classification: LCC D843 .F372 2024 (print) | LCC D843 (ebook) | DDC
    909.82/5–dc23/eng/20230701
LC record available at https://lccn.loc.gov/2023031023
LC ebook record available at https://lccn.loc.gov/2023031024

Copyright © 2024 Bearport Publishing Company. All rights reserved. No part of this publication may be reproduced in whole or in part, stored in any retrieval system, or transmitted in any form or by any means, electronic, mechanical, photocopying, recording, or otherwise, without written permission from the publisher.

For more information, write to Bearport Publishing, 5357 Penn Avenue South, Minneapolis, MN 55419.

Contents

A War of Ideas 4

From World War to Cold War 6

Two Superpowers 10

East vs. West 14

Secrets and Spies 16

The Arms Race 18

The Cold War Heats Up 22

The Wall Falls 26

Picking Sides 28

SilverTips for Success 29

Glossary 30

Read More 31

Learn More Online 31

Index 32

About the Author 32

A War of Ideas

World War II was fought with guns, planes, and bombs. Many millions of people died. Whole cities were destroyed. When it finally ended, a very different kind of war started. The United States and the Soviet Union entered the Cold War. But this fighting didn't have battlefields with tanks and soldiers.

The Soviet Union was also known as the USSR. It was a large country in Europe and Asia. What is left of the Soviet Union today is known as Russia.

From World War to Cold War

World War II lasted from 1939 until 1945. Most of the fighting took place in Europe and Asia. After the war, many countries needed to rebuild.

As most of these places started over, the United States and the Soviet Union leaped forward. They became the two most powerful countries in the world.

> The United States and the USSR were both on the winning side of the war. This gave them more power after it ended.

The United States and the Soviet Union were **allies** during World War II. They had worked together. After the war, things changed. The countries disagreed. They had different views on how the world should move forward. Soon, their relationship grew tense. The Cold War began.

The USSR wanted to take over parts of Europe that were weak after the war. But in 1948, the United States gave Europe money to rebuild. Some say this marked the start of the Cold War.

World leaders met at the end of World War II.

Two Superpowers

The United States and the Soviet Union were very different. The Soviet Union was a **communist** country. The government owned and controlled many parts of life. In the United States, people had more freedom over their things. The United States worried what would happen if more countries became communist.

The United States was a **democracy**. People picked their leaders. They voted on what they wanted to happen. The Soviet Union was a **dictatorship**. The country was run by one person with total power.

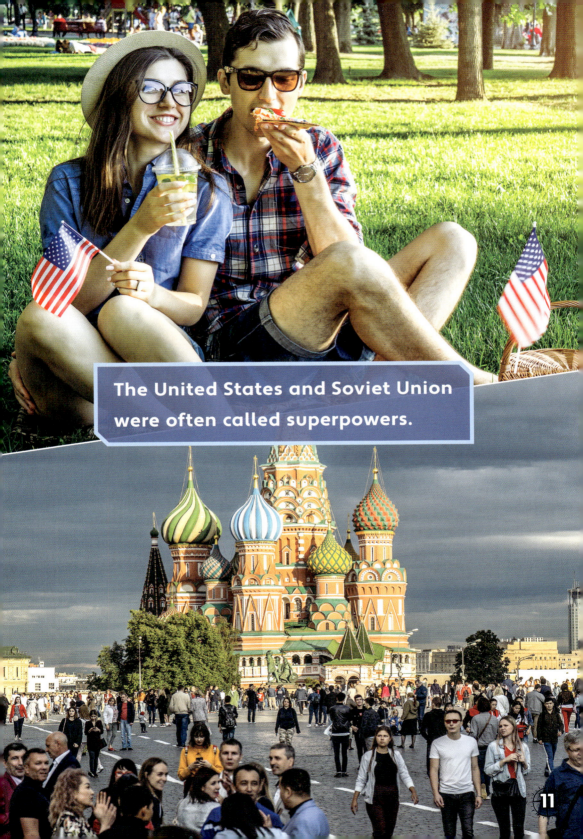

The United States and Soviet Union were often called superpowers.

Both countries wanted to spread their own way of life around the world. They also hoped to stop the other from getting more power. But after World War II, no one wanted to fight another big war. Instead, the United States and USSR used **propaganda** (prah-puh-GAN-duh) to battle for their ideas.

Cold War propaganda took many forms. Both sides used film, music, writing, and art to spread their beliefs. Propaganda was used both at home and in other countries.

East vs. West

The Cold War divided the world. The Soviet Union led the Eastern Bloc. This group included communist countries. The United States was part of the Western Bloc against communism.

As the world split, Germany was divided. So was the city of Berlin. A wall was built separating communist East Germany from West Germany.

> The border between the Western Bloc countries and the Eastern Bloc countries was called the Iron Curtain. It was difficult for people and information to cross back and forth.

Soldiers guarded the Berlin Wall.

Secrets and Spies

Not everybody agreed with the beliefs of their country. Some even **spied** for the opposite side. The U.S. and USSR governments knew this. They tried to stop people they thought might be working against their country.

The U.S. government made its people afraid of communist spies within the country. This came to be known as the Red Scare. That is because red became the color that stood for communism.

The Arms Race

Neither side in the Cold War was using weapons. However, both were getting ready in case the fighting turned physical. The United States had already used **atomic bombs** during World War II. These **nuclear** weapons made the United States powerful. The Soviet Union scrambled to catch up.

The United States had dropped two atomic bombs on Japan. These bombs killed more than 200,000 people. The use of these weapons ended World War II.

By 1949, the Soviet Union had its own atomic bomb. The **arms** race was on! The two superpowers made even more powerful weapons. People worried what would happen if the countries went to war. Their weapons could destroy all life on Earth.

Some people built shelters in case of nuclear attacks. These spaces were meant to keep people safe from harmful **radiation** during and after a blast.

The Cold War Heats Up

Tensions between the United States and the Soviet Union grew. Still, they did not attack each other directly. Instead, they entered other fights. In the 1950s and 1960s, the two countries helped different sides during major wars in Korea and Vietnam.

The Korean War and Vietnam War are sometimes called proxy wars. Fighting in these places was a proxy, or stand-in, for the battle between the United States and USSR over different ideas.

In 1961, the United States put weapons in countries close to the USSR. Then in 1962, the Soviet Union started putting nuclear missiles in Cuba. The United States was afraid the Soviets would attack from this nearby communist island. For about a month, the superpowers came close to nuclear war.

> The Cuban Missile Crisis was resolved through secret meetings. People from both sides agreed to move their missiles.

The Wall Falls

In the 1970s, the United States and Soviet Union agreed to limit the weapons they would make. Slowly, tensions between the West and East began to die down. Then in November 1989, the Berlin Wall was torn down. For many, this marked the end of the Cold War.

After the Berlin Wall fell, the Soviet Union began to break apart. The country split up. New countries formed. Russia was the biggest country left.

People in Berlin tore down the wall.

Picking Sides

The Cold War divided the world. The Eastern communist Bloc was led by the Soviet Union. The United States was joined in the Western Bloc by other countries that wanted to stop the spread of communism. Here are their allies.

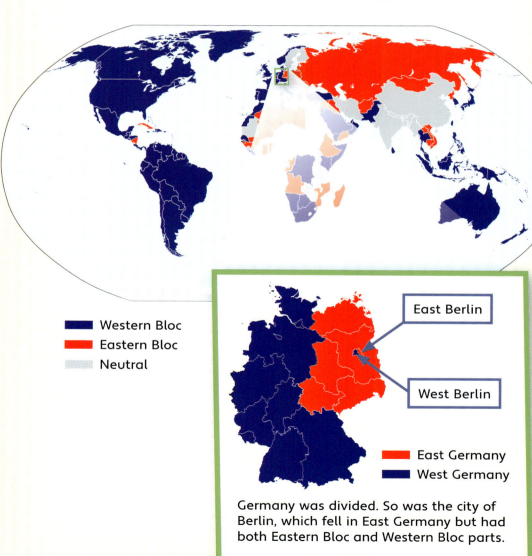

Germany was divided. So was the city of Berlin, which fell in East Germany but had both Eastern Bloc and Western Bloc parts.

SilverTips for SUCCESS

★ SilverTips for REVIEW

Review what you've learned. Use the text to help you.

Define key terms

communism
Cuban Missile Crisis
Eastern Bloc
propaganda
Western Bloc

Check for understanding

Why did the Cold War start?

What were some of the big differences between the United States and the Soviet Union during the Cold War era?

What event is considered by many to mark the end of the Cold War?

Think deeper

If the Cold War had ended differently, how do you think your life would be different today?

★ SilverTips on TEST-TAKING

- **Make a study plan.** Ask your teacher what the test is going to cover. Then, set aside time to study a little bit every day.

- **Read all the questions carefully.** Be sure you know what is being asked.

- **Skip any questions** you don't know how to answer right away. Mark them and come back later if you have time.

Glossary

allies nations that work together for a common cause, such as fighting together during a war

arms guns or other weapons that are used in a war

atomic bombs very powerful bombs that can destroy entire cities

communist a type of government where individuals do not own goods and property

democracy a form of government where the people choose leaders by voting

dictatorship a government or country where all of the power is held by one person or by a small group of people

nuclear having to do with a dangerous type of energy that produces radiation

propaganda often untrue or incomplete information that is spread to gain support for something

radiation a form of energy that can be very dangerous

spied found out secrets about someone or something using deceptive methods

Read More

Gitlin, Marty. *Postwar America (American Eras: Defining Moments).* Ann Arbor, MI: Cherry Lake Publishing, 2022.

Herschbach, Elisabeth. *Aftermath of World War II (World War II).* Lake Elmo, MN: Focus Readers, 2023.

Medina, Nico. *What Was the Berlin Wall? (What Was?).* New York: Penguin Workshop, 2019.

Learn More Online

1. Go to **www.factsurfer.com** or scan the QR code below.
2. Enter "**Cold War**" into the search box.
3. Click on the cover of this book to see a list of websites.

Index

atomic bombs 18, 20

Berlin Wall 14–15, 26–28

communism 10, 14, 16, 24, 28

Cuban Missile Crisis 24

democracy 10

dictatorship 10

Eastern Bloc 14, 28

Europe 4, 6, 8

Korean War 22

nuclear weapons 18, 20, 24

propaganda 12

spies 16

Vietnam War 22

Western Bloc 14, 28

World War II 4, 6, 8–9, 12, 18

About the Author

Daniel R. Faust is a freelance writer of fiction and nonfiction. He lives in Queens, NY.